Diets to help
CONTROL CHOLESTEROL

Cholesterol plays an important part in our metabolic processes and too little of it is as inadvisable as too much. This book describes a total nutritional approach to obtaining correct cholesterol levels and to promoting a return to health and vigour from conditions such as high blood-pressure and coronary heart disease.

Diets to Help
CONTROL
CHOLESTEROL

ROGER NEWMAN TURNER
B.Ac., N.D., D.O., M.R.O., M.R.N.

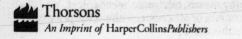
Thorsons
An Imprint of HarperCollinsPublishers

Thorsons
An Imprint of HarperCollins*Publishers*
77–85 Fulham Palace Road,
Hammersmith, London W6 8JB
1160 Battery Street,
San Francisco, California 94111–1213

First published 1978
Second edition published 1988
This edition, revised and updated, 1993
10 9 8 7 6 5

A catalogue record for this book
is available from the British Library

ISBN 0 7225 2932 5

Phototypeset by Harper Phototypesetters Limited,
Northampton, England
Printed and bound in Great Britain by
Caledonian International Book Manufacturing Ltd, Glasgow

Contents

Introduction

Epidemiology is a grand sounding name which is enjoying increasing use. It simply means the study of the incidence and distribution of disease. Apart from being a rather morbid statistical pastime, the knowledge gained about the areas where particular diseases are prevalent enables interesting correlations to be drawn regarding the diet and other social habits of a community.

A good example is the study which showed that in certain African tribes there is a complete absence of cancer of the bowel. By studying the dietary habits of these tribes it was noted that they consumed a much higher proportion of fibre than people in more 'civilized' parts of the world where bowel cancer is prevalent. Thus new corroboration of the long-held naturopathic view of the importance of fibre in the diet was gained.

By similar comparative studies important information is being gained about the role of other factors in our diet, one of which is cholesterol.

Cholesterol has been found to play a significant part in the onset of several major scourges of civilized society.

The epidemiologist can, therefore, provide information that may lead to important knowledge about the prevention of degenerative disease. One of the most widespread degenerative diseases is arteriosclerosis, or hardening of the arteries. It leads, quite often, to a common cause of death, coronary heart disease. Studies have shown that these conditions are much more prevalent in countries of the western world such as the USA, England, Scotland and Germany. All sorts of reasons could be given for this, but studies of dietary habits, and in particular the consumption of fats and carbohydrates, have been rewarding.

Various surveys in the USA and some European countries have shown a definite correlation between a high incidence of coronary heart disease and raised blood-cholesterol levels. Conversely, in some eastern countries, the average cholesterol level is low, as is the incidence of heart disease. The incidence of arteriosclerosis follows a roughly similar pattern. Post-mortem examinations of American soldiers killed in Korea during the troubles there showed a much higher incidence of arteriosclerosis by comparison with Korean soldiers. This observation naturally led to an examination of the factors which might account for the difference, foremost among which was a comparison of the dietary habits of the two races. The American youths had grown up with a diet of refined cereals, sugar, candies and cola beverages. They also had a significantly higher intake of animal fats. The Koreans, on the other hand, had used very little animal fat, existing from an early age on foods prepared in vegetable oils and having much less carbohydrate than their more 'civilized' opponents.

The same pattern has emerged from a number of comparative studies of developed and less privileged nations. This raises the question of what the normal blood-cholesterol level should be.

The amount of cholesterol in the blood is measured in milligrams per 100 millilitres of blood, the 'normal' level being given as around 180mg per 100ml. It may vary according to age and sex. But this level is based on the average, often in a westernized community, and it may by no means reflect what is a healthy level.

The difference between various groups is well illustrated by a study made in South Africa some years ago (Bronté–Stuart, *et al*, 1956) in which the mean level among Europeans was found to be 234mg/100ml, whereas that of the Bantu peoples was 166mg/100ml. Clearly the 'normal' level for people in a westernized nation may be too high for good health.

Arteriosclerosis, high blood-pressure, heart disease and gall-stones are among the most common complaints of the westernized nations and they are all associated with high serum-cholesterol levels. (Blood is composed of two parts – the cells and the plasma, or serum. The serum is the part in which cholesterol is carried and the term 'serum-cholesterol' is therefore used as well as 'blood-cholesterol'). Although there may be other characteristics of the western way of life which could account for the prevalence of some of these diseases, the dietary considerations are assuming greater importance. A close look at the dietary habits of western nations shows a predominance of fats and carbohydrates in the menu and these are the chief causes of raised cholesterol levels.

It would be unreasonable, though, to place sole responsibility for these troubles on cholesterol. Because of the link between raised cholesterol levels and the various diseases mentioned above it is a constituent of the blood and diet which has been studied more closely, but other substances are also being implicated as causative factors. The triglycerides, for example, are another group of fats that may turn out to be as important as cholesterol in weaving the pattern of disease.

When thinking about fatty foods and carbohydrates as sources of cholesterol, we should not forget that it is also produced in the body, by the liver, for the very good reason that we need it – in the right proportions. Cholesterol plays an important role in our fat absorption, is an essential constituent of the bile and helps to form the protective sheaths of the nerves, to name but a few of its functions in the body.

The rate of cholesterol production by the liver varies and it depends on the amount in the diet. The only effective way of regulating the blood-cholesterol is, therefore, by dietary control and this book aims to give uncomplicated advice on how to go about this. Each food in common use has been assessed for its cholesterol value and there are numerous books available listing them and recommending daily allowances. But dietary control of your cholesterol intake does not necessarily have to involve you in endless weighing and measuring of foods. It is far more important to understand the way in which cholesterol works in your body and how it interacts with other essential items in your diet. It is then possible to select a balanced diet, on food reform lines, in which cholesterol is automatically taken in the right proportions.

As it plays an important part in our metabolic processes a cholesterol-free diet is, in any case, inadvisable. A low-cholesterol diet can be followed but is almost useless if certain other essential nutrients are absent, for example some vitamins which help to emulsify the fats.

So, the diets to control cholesterol in this book will take into account the importance of a complete nutritional programme rather than 'low-cholesterol' for its own sake. We shall also consider in what other ways it may be possible to keep a healthy heart, blood vessels, and gall-bladder, indeed whole bodies. In this way your diets to control cholesterol will be an important and effective part of a complete return to vigorous health.

CHAPTER ONE

Natural History of Cholesterol

In the past thirty years or so cholesterol has become the 'whipping-boy' of medical nutritionists. It has been the target for all sorts of criticism, largely because of the statistical evidence that has shown high cholesterol levels in sufferers from such degenerative conditions as atherosclerosis and coronary heart disease. Blood-cholesterol is relatively easy to measure and it is, therefore, a suitable topic for study, so a great deal of research has been done on its relationship to various diseases. When this happens to any substance it begins to assume greater importance than many other more neglected factors.

But in all the attempts to incriminate cholesterol, very little is said in its defence, and it can in fact produce quite good character references. It plays a role in a wide variety of metabolic processes and, although we obtain considerable amounts of cholesterol from our diet, it is important enough to be produced by the body itself. It is found throughout the body, but is produced mainly by the liver, which provides the cholesterol required for the manufacture of certain hormones and the bile salts. Cholesterol also helps to form the protective sheaths of the nerves.

DISCOVERY OF CHOLESTEROL

Cholesterol gained its name from its association with the bile. Cholesterol means in Greek 'bile solid' and it was first isolated from gall-stones in the latter part of the eighteenth century. Its discovery in other parts of the body soon followed. Cholesterol is a sterol, or solid alcohol, which will not dissolve in water. This means that for it to be transported to those parts of the body in which it is required there must be adequate fat in which it can dissolve, that is, it is a fat-soluble substance. The nature of the fat in which cholesterol is transported is of vital importance to the freedom with which it moves in the blood.

Fats in nature are basically of two types, those that are hard at room temperature, such as butter, and those that are liquid, such as vegetable and nut oils. The harder fats, usually of animal origin, are called 'saturated' fats because in their molecular structure the chain of carbon atoms is linked to the hydrogen atoms. This gives stability to the atoms and hardness to the fat, which are then less easy to break down in the body. The molecular structure of the unsaturated fats, on the other hand, is more flexible because there are fewer hydrogen atoms linked to the carbon ones. Where there is more than one free carbon atom the molecule is called a 'polyunsaturated fat' such as sunflower seed oil.

CHOLESTEROL AND FATS

Cholesterol combines with fats to become a cholesterol ester, which is the form in which it is carried around the body. But cholesterol can combine much more readily with unsaturated than with saturated fats and it is important that the relative proportions of these is maintained at a correct level in the diet. Too much of the foods such as butter, cream and eggs may flood the bloodstream with the saturated fats. Cholesterol will have difficulty in combining with these and there will be a corresponding rise of its level in the blood. This always happens after a fatty meal.

There are several types of cholesterol, some good, some bad. The good cholesterol is known as high density lipoprotein (HDL) and the less healthy type is low density lipoprotein (LDL). It is important to keep a higher ratio of HDL to LDL in the blood.

A diet which is regularly high in saturated hard fats (i.e. LDL) will soon lead to a chronically raised blood-cholesterol level with some of the consequences referred to in the introduction, for example arteriosclerosis and heart disease.

STABILIZING CHOLESTEROL

A further complication of high intake of animal fats is inadequate secretion of bile. Bile flow is better promoted by unsaturated fats and when bile flows smoothly more cholesterol is secreted and less accumulates in the blood. Besides, the bile acids aid the digestion of fats.

When the significance of the blood-cholesterol level was appreciated the normal level in healthy subjects had to be determined. This could only be done by taking the average in selected population groups. But the subjects selected for these readings might not all have been healthy. Even if they were at the time of testing, could their cholesterol level be relied upon to be a guide if they were heading for arteriosclerosis or gall-bladder trouble? In fact since the records of cholesterol levels have been kept the average has crept up. In the 1920s the normal level was around 160mg/100ml. By the 1950s it had reached 190mg, undoubtedly a reflection of the change in eating habits during that time. These figures relate only to the United Kingdom.

There must obviously be some sort of regulatory mechanism which maintains fairly constant levels of cholesterol when dietary intake varies so much. One of the main ways in which the body disposes of excess cholesterol is in the secretion of bile acids. An adequate amount of unsaturated fat is necessary in the diet to maintain regular bile flow.

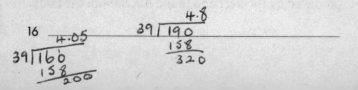

FIBRE

Further excretion depends on adequate bowel function and therefore the fibre content of your diet is of vital importance. Fibre is also necessary to maintain correct intestinal bacteria. The bacterial flora assist in the breakdown of cholesterol to coprosterol which is excreted in the faeces.

A number of other factors regulate the cholesterol level, among the more important of which are the presence of other nutrients. There are many vitamins and minerals which interact with each other to regulate body chemistry. That is why a healthy diet contains foods which provide a wide variety of these substances.

ROLE OF THE VITAMINS

Several vitamins play a vital role in the cholesterol metabolism, either directly or indirectly. Vitamin B12, for example, accelerates the flow of bile salts. Other vitamins are necessary, in particular choline, which promotes cholesterol utilization in the tissues, the conversion of fats to yield energy and excretion via the bile.

The ease with which fats dissolve in the bloodstream depends on the sufficiency of choline, which is the active constituent of lecithin. Lecithin, a group of substances known as the phospholipids, is produced by the liver and found throughout the body, especially in nerve and brain cells. Its importance to fat metabolism is paramount because it aids the breakdown of fats and cholesterol to the microscopic particles which can be carried in suspension in the blood. The work of lecithin is, in turn, made easier by the presence of vitamin E, which also greatly reduces the oxygen requirements of the tissues, so offsetting the ill effects of restricted circulation when this is due to fatty deposits or other causes.

Cholesterol is essential for the synthesis of certain hormones, particularly the steroids (e.g. cortizone), produced by the adrenal glands, the sex hormones and the pituitary hormones. These, in their turn, affect the blood levels of fats and cholesterol. The thyroid gland, for example, which like other glands is under the influence of the pituitary, secretes a hormone which lowers the blood-lipid level.

YOUR GENES AND CHOLESTEROL

Our resilience or susceptibility to disease is, to some extent, determined by heredity. Modern research into genetic influences on disease has discovered that the tendency to manufacture large amounts of cholesterol may be inherited. This condition, known as Familial hypercholesterolaemia (FH), affects a small percentage of the population.

People with FH have much more difficulty in

lowering the cholesterol levels because the body is programmed to produce more than it needs. They are often prescribed cholesterol-lowering drugs, but it is particularly important for them to follow the dietary advice given in this book to minimize the production of cholesterol. Nutritional supplements are also an essential part of the programme for the person with FH.

If your parents, grandparents, or other close relatives suffered from arteriosclerosis, high blood-pressure, heart attacks, or strokes, it would be wise to have your cholesterol levels checked regularly.

Another gene, the apo-lipo B gene, helps us to deal with cholesterol more effectively. It has been found that when this gene is defective, even people with normal cholesterol levels may be more susceptible to coronary heart disease than those with higher levels.

Fortunately, reducing the risk factors for heart disease, arteriosclerosis and stroke, coupled with a wholefood diet rich in protective nutrients, offers the most effective way of dealing with these inherited defects.

In chapter 6 we shall take a closer look at some of these vitamins and minerals and how they may be included in the diet, but first you should understand more about the importance of controlling cholesterol levels.

CHAPTER TWO

Why Control Cholesterol?

With all the important functions performed by cholesterol you would think that we couldn't get too much of it from our diet. Abundant cholesterol would surely mean better bile salts and fat digestion, better protected nerves and adequate hormones to meet the body's crises. But the body physiology and chemistry are complex and the interrelationship of different nutrients is so intricate as to be understood at only a very superficial level. Also the epidemiologists have produced so much information to confirm that we obviously can get too much cholesterol and that the long-term consequences can be quite serious.

Arteriosclerosis and coronary heart disease are two of the greatest ravages of the western world. Their cost in terms of life and human potential is immeasurable. Very often, by the time they become evident, they are quite well advanced and the general decline in vitality and mental faculties is irreversible.

ARTERIOSCLEROSIS

This decline is particularly so with arteriosclerosis, which is a gradual thickening of the inner linings of the arteries. Examined microscopically they show raised yellow streaks. Extra cells are laid down which are distended with droplets of fat and cholesterol, and these thicken the walls. As these spread the lumen of the arteries becomes narrow and it loses its elasticity with the formation of fibrous tissue and calcium deposits. Blood flow is impeded and the reduction of circulation to the part of the body affected brings about a gradual deterioration in the vitality of the cells.

In the legs, the lack of sufficient oxygen may cause cramp and severe pain in the muscles. In the brain, undernourished nerve cells gradually die and memory or other mental faculties decline. In the heart the obstruction of blood supply to a sufficiently large area of the muscle can bring about the fatal heart attack. No previous evidence of ill health may have been apparent. Those young American servicemen killed in Korea, who were found to have arteriosclerosis, would have been likely candidates for early heart attacks had they survived to return to their rich western diets.

Arteriosclerosis may lead to a variety of other disorders including high blood-pressure, kidney disease and diabetes.

There is not much one can do about a gradual erosion of health of this sort if one is not aware that it is taking place. But we do know some of the things which affect our cholesterol levels. Certain ones we have no control over, but others, such as diet, we do. There is evidence that some of the degenerative changes of arteriosclerosis can be reversed by the adoption of a suitable diet.

OTHER CAUSES

If, for any reason, your blood cholesterol has been measured and found to be in excess of 200mg/100ml you may have already taken steps to reduce it. But even if it is normal it is as well to remember that other factors may contribute to heart disease or gall-bladder troubles. We don't yet know, for certain, that cholesterol is the chief culprit; raised blood levels of other fats, such as the triglycerides, are also significant causes of these disorders. The selection of a low-cholesterol diet with food reform principles in mind can also have the necessary regulatory control over these other nutritional factors.

The correlation between raised blood-cholesterol and heart disease has been repeatedly emphasized by many authors. In fact the message is evidently getting through because in the USA there has recently been a decline in the number of deaths from coronary thrombosis. The death rate has fallen by 13 per cent since 1960 and the average American's blood-cholesterol level has dropped between 5 and 10 per cent during the same period. Figures from the Federal

Department of Agriculture show that from 1963 to 1973 there was a 57 per cent decrease in the consumption of animal fats and a 44.1 per cent increase in the intake of vegetable oils.

Two important points emerge from this. Firstly, the reduction of hard animal fats emphasizes the relationship between these and heart disease, but, secondly, the increase in the use of vegetable oils is also significant. These are the unsaturated fats which keep cholesterol in solution and prevent the furring of the arteries.

VARIATIONS OF CHOLESTEROL LEVEL

The blood-cholesterol level remains fairly constant throughout the day but is subject to variations within a normal range according to age, sex, exercise and other habits such as smoking. The mean cholesterol level tends to rise steadily with advancing years in the male, but in the female it shows a slight reduction in levels during the years of active menstruation, followed by a slight elevation after the menopause. This is due to hormone fluctuations. Oestrogen produced during the menstrual cycle tends to lower cholesterol levels. In pregnancy, the serum-cholesterol rises temporarily due to the natural reduction of the hormone.

Exercise certainly keeps the blood-cholesterol level

down. Some nomadic tribes in Africa have a mean blood-cholesterol level of only 166mg/100ml, in spite of a diet that is rich in animal fats. This is probably due to the exercise they get following their herds.

CONSEQUENCES OF NO EXERCISE

Our bodies were made to undertake far more exercise than most of us get in our everyday lives and, as nature is economical, muscles that are no longer used quickly waste. Those that have previously been developed by athletic pursuits and are then neglected degenerate to fatty tissue. Tissues that do not have the stimulus of exercise to promote circulation quickly lose vitality and become prone to infection and the kind of degeneration that includes a rise in cholesterol levels.

Another consequence of inadequate exercise is constipation. The sluggishness of intestinal activity allows more time for bile to be reabsorbed into the bloodstream and, with it, more cholesterol.

Other insidious poisons can lower health and resistance, such as the chemicals used in, and on, many foods. Avoid these as much as possible, using organically grown food which is free of insecticides and sprays during its growth.

PREVENTION IS BEST

It should be increasingly evident that the regulation of cholesterol levels is a matter not just of therapeutic necessity, but of essential prevention. A diet that maintains low cholesterol levels, and promotes a healthier metabolism all round, is necessary for everyone long before the raised levels are detected. Remember that by the time the blood tests are done, degenerative changes can be quite well advanced. But diets to control cholesterol don't have to be chapters of deprivation. What is called for is an understanding of how the right or wrong combinations of foods affect cholesterol levels.

CHAPTER THREE

How Diet Affects Cholesterol Levels

Mathematics and nutrition should never be mixed. One of the great dangers of a preoccupation with figures is that the diets prepared on the basis of them carry a greater risk than the food they seek to restrict. People drive themselves crazy counting calories, weighing 'average servings' and trying to restrict their sodium intake to so many milligrams per day. In practice very few people have the time or the patience to do this and they either lose interest rapidly or they work out a diet low in cholesterol, or whatever, but thoroughly unhealthy in other ways.

So, rather than go through the tedium of weighing foods and measuring their cholesterol levels, it is far more important to aim for a well-balanced diet, whilst ensuring that it is low in the obvious cholesterol-raisers. And to ensure that what cholesterol you do have is kept in solution, the diet must have adequate supplies of the foods that help to dissolve it – the unsaturated fats and abundant natural vitamins.

FAT DIGESTION

Once fats in the food enter the duodenum, just below the stomach, their digestion can begin. The bile salts secreted by the liver and stored in the gall-bladder break down the fats and cholesterol to small globules which can be absorbed into a system of ducts, called the lacteals, and thence to the bloodstream. These fat globules, or chilomicrons, are of varying sizes depending on the efficiency with which they are broken down. The harder animal fats are high in saturated fatty acids and form large particles. The unsaturated fatty acids are more readily broken down to finer globules and can be better absorbed. For cholesterol, or any of the saturated fats, to be utilized the diet must contain certain unsaturated fatty acids; linolenic, linoleic and arachidonic acids. These are known as the Essential Fatty Acids (EFAs). Linolenic acid must be provided in the diet, but the others can be synthesized by the body as long as adequate nutrients are provided. Sunflower and soya oil are the richest sources of the EFAs.

A number of research workers have shown that the cholesterol level can be reduced by substituting vegetable oils for animal fats in the diet. There is extra evidence in the comparison between the average cholesterol levels of westernized communities, where 40 per cent of the calories are derived from fats, and those of the less prosperous nations, whose fat intake is 20 per cent less.

LECITHIN

There are other emulsifiers in the diet and one of the most important of these is lecithin, or the phospholipids. These aid the transport of fats by keeping them in solution. A major source of lecithin in the diet is eggs, and egg yolk also happens to be one of the richest sources of cholesterol. Eggs are generally excluded in low-cholesterol diets, but whilst they must be controlled, they may be taken in a very limited quantity, to provide lecithin, by those whose cholesterol level is not unduly high. Lecithin is also found in vegetable oils, such as those derived from soya and sunflower. 'To egg or not to egg' depends on whether prevention or cure of high cholesterol is your aim.

Eggs, however, raise the question of animal protein in general. All animal protein, with the exception of fish, is high in saturated fatty acids, apart from which meat is rather too toxic for human consumption on a regular basis, since our digestive system is not physiologically adapted to a carnivorous diet. Undoubtedly, a low-fat vegetarian diet is healthiest, but for those who find it hard to do without meats, the lean types are best. This is better than a vegetarian diet high in proteins from eggs and cheese, which of course contain more cholesterol. Fish, on the other hand, tends to be low in saturated fats and has components that emulsify cholesterol.

CARBOHYDRATES

The relationship between animal fats and high blood-cholesterol is well known. In fact there is a danger that people suffering from the cholesterol-induced diseases, such as gall-stones and arteriosclerosis, may severely curtail their fat intake but fill up on sweet or starchy foods – the carbohydrates. Carbohydrates, especially the refined ones, such as white flour, sugar and some breakfast foods, are almost as important a cause of raised cholesterol as the animal fats, but there are lots of beneficial carbohydrates that contain the whole grain, such as oats, wheat, and rice.

Sugar and white flour are such concentrated forms of carbohydrate – they have had most of their fibre together with essential nutrients found in the natural state removed from them – that they tend to be absorbed much more rapidly than the digestive system can cope with. Over a period of some years this puts an intolerable strain on the secretions of the various digestive enzymes with consequences that can range from headaches, fatigue and irritability, through constipation, gall-stones and indigestion, to diabetes, high blood-pressure and heart disease. Lying behind many of these problems will be a high blood-cholesterol level.

Constipation can arise for several reasons. Deficiency of bile secretion is one of them since bile salts facilitate an easier bowel action. The lack of fibre and roughage, though, is an even greater cause of constipation, and without fibre the intestinal bacteria, which break down excess cholesterol to coprosterol for elimination in the faeces, cannot function normally.

The grossly inadequate advice on diet that is given to most sufferers from the diseases mentioned here undoubtedly contributes to some of the fatalities for which they are responsible. The proper integration of the various elements of a natural diet is of vital importance to the victim of high blood-cholesterol. It is just as important for the rest of us to tailor our diets for prevention.

CHAPTER FOUR

Tailoring Your Diet for Prevention

You may be reading this book because you are unfortunate enough to have a high cholesterol level or one of the disorders associated with it. Actually, if your raised cholesterol level was discovered in good time, you are fortunate rather than unfortunate, because many people are not aware of it until they have a stroke or heart attack.

You may, on the other hand, wish to take steps now to prevent the build up of what can only lead to a declining mental and physical vitality as the years go by.

Perhaps there is a history of high blood-pressure or heart disease in your family. These are not inherited automatically, only the tendency to them, and you would then certainly be wise to take preventive measures. Look upon it not just as prevention, but as health improvement in a positive way. A revision of your diet to incorporate the food reform principles outlined here will do far more for your general well-being than simply control your cholesterol level.

MAKING A CHANGE

If you have been accustomed to a 'normal' diet, one in which convenience foods, white flour, sugar and animal fats featured prominently, you may not find it easy to change. Adopting a healthy diet takes time and effort, and means sacrificing a good many pleasures, particularly if you have a sweet tooth! But it is surprising how many good alternatives can be found and in time you will wonder how you ever managed to eat the conventional rubbish.

We all have our personal idiosyncrasies when it comes to diet, so, bearing in mind the basic principles, it is wise to adapt the suggestions given here to suit yours. But don't be afraid to give your idiosyncrasies a good kick. They may well have been based on a false premise. Perhaps some food was blamed for upsetting your system, when the real fault lay with the functional weakness in your digestive organs. People with a history of gastric ulcers or diverticulosis, for example, often studiously avoid fresh raw fruit and vegetables, the very foods they require to provide fibre and vital elements which will strengthen and heal their devitalized and pampered guts.

FOOD SELECTION

In setting about the selection of a new menu it is as well to have a clear idea of the high-cholesterol foods, which should be avoided, as well as those that provide the essential fatty acids to emulsify fats and carry the fat-soluble vitamins to different parts of the body. If the diet is on food-reform principles it will almost automatically be a low-cholesterol and low-calorie diet, so with a little knowledge of the categories in which foods belong, a lot of the sweat of cholesterol and calorie counting can be avoided.

We have already discussed, in earlier chapters, the classes of foods that provide cholesterol and those that are liable to raise the level of it in the blood when taken in excess. They are, you will recall, the hard or saturated fats and refined carbohydrates. Now we shall consider the sorts of food in the normal diet that contain these basic ingredients.

Foods that contain large amounts of the saturated fats will certainly have to be excluded from the diets of those with high cholesterol levels. If you are adopting a prevention programme you will still need to exclude them from your daily menu though they might be permitted on that 'special occasion' – provided that the diet has sufficient natural emulsifiers to cope with the extra fat. Certainly, some self-discipline and sacrifice will be necessary, but for most of the exclusions there are good alternatives to which your palate can quickly become accustomed. As we have learned so much about them let us begin with the fats.

FATS AND OILS

Exclude	In moderation	Allowed
Animal fats, lard, etc.	Vegetable oil margarines	Sunflower oil
Butter	hydrogenated oils	Safflower oil
Cream	(sunflower or	Corn oil
Mayonnaise	safflower	Nuts
Nuts high in saturated fats, e.g. cashews, brazils	margarine is best)	containing polyunsaturated fats, e.g. walnuts and almonds

Butter or Margarine?

Although butter is commonly condemned in the world of cholesterol control because of its high content of saturated fat, many of the commercially available margarines may not be much better. The vegetable oils from which they are made are subjected to a process of hardening, known as hydrogenation, to make them solid at room temperature. This renders the fat into a form that is almost as difficult to digest as butter. There are one or two brands of margarine that do not use this process. Ask at your health food store about these.

Moderation with all hard fats must be the rule and

if you use vegetable oil margarines regularly be sure to take extra vitamin E, which helps to emulsify the fat (see chapter 6).

DAIRY FOODS

Exclude	In moderation	Allowed
Butter	Sunflower oil margarine	Plant milk substitutes
Whole milk	Skimmed milk or buttermilk	Almond cream
Fatty cheeses, e.g. Brie and Camembert	Low-fat cheese	Cottage cheese
Processed cheese	Water ices	Skimmed milk cheeses
Cream		
Eggs		
Ice cream		

MEAT AND FISH

It is preferable to exclude all meat or fish, but for those who find this difficult and for whom regular protein intake is important (e.g. hypoglycaemic people), the following controls should be exercised.

Exclude	In moderation	Allowed
Fatty meats	All organ meats	Lean meats
Duck	Poultry (free range	Fresh fish
Game	only)	
Pork		
Kidney		
Tongue		
Shell fish		

GRAINS AND CEREAL FOODS

Exclude	In moderation	Allowed
White flour and all foods made with it, e.g. bread, cakes, biscuits, pies	Cereals prepared with whole grains and natural ingredients	Wholemeal flour and bread
All other refined cereals, e.g. white rice, cornflour and breakfast cereals		Wheatgerm
		Bran
		Oatmeal
		Brown rice
		Millet
		Buckwheat
		Whole wheat
		Whole maize
		Couscous

SWEETS AND TREATS

Exclude	In moderation	Allowed
Sugar, white or brown	Honey	Fresh or dried fruits
Sweets	Maple syrup	Stewed fruit – sweetened with honey
Chocolates	Molasses	
Glucose and all other concentrated sweeteners	Dried fruit slices or other snacks containing natural ingredients	Home-baked produce using wholemeal flour and natural ingredients, e.g. vegetable oils, honey
Cakes, biscuits, pastries		
Custards, jams		
All artificially flavoured jellies, puddings, ice-creams		Seaweed-based jellies and blanc-manges e.g. carrageen
Saccharine and other artificial sweeteners		

RESTORING YOUR SENSE OF TASTE

The first impression you might get from these tables is that the ground of good taste and convenience has been cut from under your gastronomic feet. But this is far from being the case. Certainly the restriction of many canned and packaged products will make a little more work, but the improvement in taste will more than repay the effort.

The true taste of many canned and packaged foods is masked by the salt, sugar and other preservatives which are, in any case, harmful to the sufferer from cholesterol-related diseases. Once you have got used to eating more fresh, unadulterated foods, the sensitivity of your taste-buds, dulled by years of salt and sugar, from the cradle onwards, will return and open whole new territories of taste experience for you.

Some of the exclusions and modifications are based, not only on high cholesterol content, but on their harmfulness in other ways, such as foods with a high sodium content. Your health is not just a question of one nutritional ingredient, but of the whole spectrum of dietary and other factors.

Working out a diet on low-cholesterol lines may take a little time. The menu needs to be planned to give adequate protein throughout the day, whilst also providing plenty of vegetable fibre and whole grains for roughage. It needn't be too difficult if you keep in mind the following rules:

GENERAL RULES FOR DIETS TO CONTROL CHOLESTEROL

1 The major proportion of the diet is to consist of fresh fruit and vegetables, eaten raw whenever possible. Approximate proportions should be fruit and vegetables 65 per cent, proteins 20 per cent, carbohydrates 15 per cent. Fruit and vegetables, of course, contain proteins and carbohydrates and there is some protein in whole-grain carbohydrates, so the overlap of all components ensures more than adequate intake.

2 Whenever possible all foods should be organically grown and prepared without the use of synthetic additives, preservatives and flavouring agents. Try to find a nursery, or greengrocer, whose produce is grown without artificial fertilizers and pesticides and obtain your other requirements at a health food store.

3 Use the conservative method of cooking vegetables to avoid destroying vitamins and leaching minerals more than necessary. This means using a little water in the bottom of the saucepan and cooking the vegetables until just tender. Add further water if it boils dry. The vegetables taste so much better when prepared this way. Don't pressure cook as this destroys enzymes and essential nutrients in the foods. A microwave oven should be used only when essential and not as a regular method of cooking.

4 Sprouting grains and seeds is an excellent way to increase their nutritional properties. Health food stores sell grain sprouters in which such foods as wheat, sesame seeds, alfalfa and some beans can be sprouted. The seeds or grains are spread on trays and water is rinsed through them daily until the shoots are half to one inch high. Serve the whole seeds and sprouts with salads or use in sandwiches.

5 For improved digestion it is better not to drink with meals. Limit drinks to between meals, except perhaps a small vegetable or fruit juice aperitif. There will be ample liquid in your diet when you have fresh salads and fruits regularly.

6 Always eat meals in a quiet, restful atmosphere. Endeavour to have your evening meal early enough to allow for digestion before retiring. Do not eat large meals at any time, but particularly when overtired or tense.

With these guidelines in mind it is possible to consider a basic menu for cholesterol control along the following lines.

BASIC MENU

On Rising

Warm water, lemon juice and honey drink; or apple cider vinegar and honey drink; or fresh fruit juice (e.g.

apple, grape, orange, pineapple or canned or bottled unsweetened juices).

Breakfast

Fresh fruit, such as apples, pears, grapes, peaches, pineapple, bananas, oranges, melons, blackcurrants, plums; or soaked dried fruits, such as apricots or prunes; or a fruit salad containing a selection of these fruits sprinkled with nuts, raisins, wheat germ, and topped with goat's milk yogurt.

Alternatively, baked, stewed or puréed apple with raisins, sprinkled with nuts or wheat germ; or home-made muesli with wheat germ, topped with yogurt, skimmed milk or soya milk; or porridge served with soya or skimmed milk, and wheat germ.

If desired, finish with one or two slices of wholemeal toast or brown rye biscuits with sunflower oil margarine and honey, or a low-sodium savoury spread such as vegetable or yeast extracts.

Breakfast drinks may consist of herb teas, china tea, or a suitable cereal beverage, or coffee substitute, or dandelion coffee. Use soya milk or other plant-based milk substitute, or skimmed milk, with the beverages. Herb teas should be taken without addition of milk, but with a slice of lemon if preferred.

Between Meals

For drinks between meals use the same as above, or fresh or bottled fruit juices. The savoury extracts or spread can also be used in hot water as a drink. Use only a little honey to sweeten drinks where this is necessary.

If a light snack is desired it should consist of a few nuts or sunflower seeds or perhaps some raisins or a little fresh fruit or biscuits made with low-cholesterol ingredients.

Mid-day Meal

As an aperitif a small glass of fruit or vegetable juice. The lactofermented juices are particularly well tolerated and beneficial. Use beetroot, carrot, celery or mixed juices.

Combination salad containing a selection of vegetables in season. Salads should be possible every day of the year but vary the recipes for variety. Choose from lettuce, endive, chicory, cabbage, watercress, Chinese cabbage, celery, cucumber, beetroot, tomato, onion, garlic and others. All these can be eaten raw but the coarser ingredients should be grated or chopped finely. Add cottage cheese or other low-fat cheeses, raisins and other fresh fruit such as grapes or apples to give flavour. Garnish with herbs as available.

Use a home-made salad dressing or simply add sunflower-seed oil.

Salad can be eaten with a serving of brown savoury rice, millet or baked jacket potato, or with two slices of brown rye biscuit or wholemeal bread.

For dessert eat some fresh fruit in season or a fruit salad or other dish with fruit according to the recipes given in chapter 7. Natural fruit jellies or seaweed-based junkets may be taken, or a goat's milk yogurt with natural fruit juice added for flavour (avoid the commercial, sweetened types).

Afternoon

Drinks as above and also light snack if desired.

Evening Meal

Hors-d'oeuvres of fresh fruit, avocado pear or vegetable soup.

The main course should be a savoury dish made with whole grains such as brown rice, millet, couscous or buckwheat, or with pulses, such as the various types of beans. Other vegetable savouries made with low-fat ingredients may be used. Serve with two or three conservatively cooked vegetables or potatoes baked in their jackets. If there is a grain dish, potato will not be required. This would provide too much carbohydrate in one meal.

For dessert use fresh or dried fruit; or fruit salad; or carrageen mould or natural fruit jelly. Any of these may be served with milled nuts and wheat germ and topped with goat's milk yogurt.

On Retiring

Apples or grapes, if food is required. A warm drink of herb tea or cereal coffee may be taken.

The mid-day and evening meals may be transposed if desired or you may take a salad at both meals when vegetables are plentiful. If it is not convenient to have a salad at mid-day because of your work, take sandwiches of wholemeal bread containing some of the ingredients. If this is not convenient take fresh fruit and some nuts or sunflower seeds.

Instead of meals of fruit, a whole day each week or two on fruit can be useful as part of the programme of cholesterol reduction and this will be one of the stricter measures we shall consider in the next chapter.

CHAPTER FIVE

Reducing the Risk

It is in our nature to face new challenges. The sense of achievement in conquering new peaks makes all the danger involved in doing it worthwhile. A lot of people get a thrill from the hazards of some activities, be it climbing mountains, or speeding on high-power motorcycles. The chances of killing themselves are high. There are many more who are taking a chance with their lives without getting the thrills. They are what I call the 'risk-takers'.

The risk-takers are the people whose dietary habits and way of life make them likely candidates for high cholesterol levels and the killer diseases associated with them. They are the eaters of rich foods, the fat takers, who often rush their meals down in combinations which present the greatest difficulty to their poor digestive organs. They are the people who live under 'pressure'. Pressure from time, pressure from business, pressure from the strain of emotional relationships – the stresses that predispose to these killer diseases. They are the people who take little regular exercise to expand their lungs and work their heart, unless it is running for the train. Faulty diet, stress and inadequate exercise all contribute directly or indirectly to a raised serum-cholesterol.

There is yet another category of risk-taker, and these are the people who have a family history of heart attacks or circulatory disorders.

All these people may be gambling against even greater odds than might appear from the thrill of their high-pressure lives. The process of decline in vitality, gradual elevation of cholesterol levels and the accumulation of other factors which make up the lethal cocktail of sudden death or a stroke occurs so slowly and insidiously that there may be no advance warning of the blow. Only by regular tests can these people know whether their blood-cholesterol level is climbing towards the danger mark. They may have headaches, and feel 'out of sorts', to warn them of the possibility of high blood-pressure. They may have legs which ache on exertion, warning them of possible blockage in the arteries or arteriosclerosis. But before any of these tell-tale symptoms occur, the risk-takers should review their diet and way of life and take special steps to reduce the risk.

A PERMANENT PLAN

The biggest and most effective step to be taken is to adopt the low-cholesterol diet as a permanent way of life. With this as the basic format for your eating habits there should be plenty of variety and interest but also the added assurance that you are taking a major step in preventive nutrition. Once cholesterol levels are raised, they don't come down quickly. It takes some weeks of well-regulated diet, coupled with an intake of special emulsifying nutrients, to reduce the level. But if you are one of the risk-takers you should consider certain other steps to reduce the odds against you.

WATCH YOUR WEIGHT

Do you, for example, need to lose weight? Overweight people run a greater risk of heart disease and diabetes. Women who are overweight, particularly those who have had children, have a higher incidence of gall-stones. The combination of obesity and high blood-cholesterol puts the person well into the high-risk category. Following the low-cholesterol diet can help to reduce both factors.

The diet suggested in chapter 4 is low on calories (approximately 1200 to 1500 calories). Just as cholesterol measurements are an unnecessary tedium for the dieter, so calorie counting is equally futile. Far more important is to ensure that the diet is balanced and wholesome. When it is, calories certainly look after themselves, cholesterol and other hard fats are generally well limited, and weight begins to reduce.

Perhaps you have been neglecting to take sufficient exercise. Do you regularly make your lungs and heart work to their limits by some brisk walking? A daily stint of jogging – even only ten minutes around the block – can just get you panting sufficiently to make the heart muscles work and the lungs expand to their fullest capacity. It will also burn up some of those calories.

The high-risk person, and certainly the one whose cholesterol level is known to be above the normal limit, does need to make some extra effort to help to get things back to healthier figures – shape as well as quantity! There are a number of other measures that can be adopted.

Firstly there are some stricter dietary disciplines, which can be followed quite easily for short spells. They require that little extra self-discipline, but the benefits and sense of well-being far outweigh the sacrifices.

THE FRUIT DAY

The easiest is to introduce a Fruit Day into your weekly dietary plan. On this day you have no other food but fresh fruit and fruit juice. Of course there is no cholesterol and very few calories on this day, so it gives your system a sort of holiday, a day in which to rest a little from the effort of digesting fats, carbohydrates and proteins.

Your fruit day will become a wonderfully refreshing experience and you will soon look forward to it each week. You may have a reasonable quantity, to satisfy your appetite, of any fresh fruit meal times. Choose from

- grapes
- apples
- pears
- oranges
- melons
- peaches
- grapefruit
- plums
- pawpaws
- avocados
- bananas

according to season and availability.

Give yourself variety and don't spend the whole day on the same fruit, especially bananas, which have a high starch content. You may, however, benefit by taking primarily grapes (the white Almeria ones are best) and/or apples for the full day. This type of mono-diet is particularly beneficial for heart disorders with fluid retention.

Citrus fruits should also be eaten in moderation. This is a caution of particular importance for the sufferer from rheumatic troubles and is worth including here because of the widespread incidence of these disorders. The Fruit Day will be of great benefit to the rheumatism sufferer in every other respect.

Between meals you may drink water, mineral water and pure unsweetened fruit juices. If a warm drink is desired a savoury yeast or vegetable extract is permitted. One teaspoonful in a mug of hot water makes a pleasant beverage. A cider-vinegar and honey drink is a good alternative. There will, however, be less desire for liquid as the water content of the fruit you eat will make up for this.

A fruit day restores the sense of taste and the feeling of clarity, although on the first few times you do it you may experience some hunger and perhaps slight headache and coated tongue. The hunger will soon go as your body adapts to the different type of nourishment. The other symptoms are normal signs of the detoxification process in operation. They too will soon go but may be regarded as an encouraging sign.

THE NEXT STAGE

When you have become accustomed to regular fruit days you will be ready for a further step in the cholesterol reduction programme. This is the Seven Day Cleansing Diet.

The cleansing diet is so named because it has a beneficial detoxifying effect on the whole system. It entails a longer period of abstinence from fats and carbohydrates, which encourages the body to draw on its reserves of these nutrients and eventually lower the levels in the blood.

In order to get your metabolism effectively launched on this seven-day programme, you should commence with a twenty-four-hour fast. The fast really stimulates a good eliminative response. The most convenient time to commence your fast will be after your evening meal, perhaps at the start of a weekend when you can rest and get the full benefit of the first three strict days.

The twenty-four-hour fast is followed by two days on fresh raw fruit and then, during the last four days, more interest is added to the diet in the form of salads and light savouries. The first three or four days may bring out the eliminative crisis of headache, coated tongue, hunger and perhaps bowel looseness. All these will pass and you will soon feel much clearer, brighter, and more energetic. Your improved senses will bring a new pleasure in the taste of the salads and vegetable dishes you will introduce as the week goes on. There will be an added relish in the return to your low-cholesterol basic diet. The seven-day programme should be as follows:

SEVEN DAY CLEANSING DIET

FIRST 24 HOURS

Fast day. Take only plain water or mineral water. Or as an alternative you may drink apple or grape juice. Four to six tumblersful may be taken during the day mainly at the normal meal times.

SECOND AND THIRD DAYS

Fresh fruit. Take as much as the appetite demands of any fresh fruit, as for the Fruit Day. The harder fruits may be chopped or grated and made into a fruit salad if desired. This can be moistened with a little fruit juice and sweetened if necessary with a teaspoonful of honey.

Between meals drink pure fruit juice or water.

FOURTH DAY

Breakfast

Fresh fruit.

Lunch

Mixed vegetable salad using ingredients as listed in chapter 4 (basic diet) or from recipes (chapter 7).

Fresh fruit as dessert.

Evening Meal

Mixed salad again or fresh fruit.

FIFTH TO SEVENTH DAYS

Breakfast

Fresh fruit as before, but if made into a fruit salad you may now add a tablespoonful of wheat germ and some sunflower seeds to provide protein. This may be topped with goat's milk yogurt.

Lunch

Mixed vegetable salad. Add dried fruit, milled nuts or wheat germ. Use a dressing made with sunflower seed oil and cider-vinegar or lemon juice.

Fresh fruit for dessert.

Evening Meal

Mixed salad as before. You may now add a little cottage cheese or a small portion of savoury rice or millet prepared according to the recipes.

Fresh fruit as dessert.

Drinks between meals should be pure fruit juice or warm savoury or cider-vinegar drinks.

HELPING BOWEL FUNCTION

As elimination is such an important part of this regime it is important to see that the bowel function continues normally. It usually will with the high proportion of fibre in the diet. On the second day, however, it will be beneficial to take a small warm-water enema, particularly if there has been no normal evacuation.

Use the gravity-feed type enema and fill the can with one or two pints of warm water at body temperature. Administer the enema in the knee-chest position allowing the water to flow slowly into the rectum. Then hold it for five minutes whilst lying on the back and gently kneading the abdomen, before evacuation.

The value of the enema is that it encourages elimination of waste matter which may not normally be evacuated with the faeces.

If you have carried out the Fruit Days regularly and undertaken the Seven Day Cleansing Diet at least once (you may need to repeat it after an interval of one or two months), you will be well on your way to healthier cholesterol levels and better vitality all round. You can assist your metabolism still further by the use of some of the special substances which nature has provided.

CHAPTER SIX

Supplementing Your Diet

Having adjusted your daily diet to reduce those foods that tend to generate the unhealthy type of cholesterol, you can help yourself still more by applying nutritional knowledge to the task of getting blood fats back to a healthy balance. There are two major prongs to this process: incorporating foods with the ability to assist in cholesterol regulation and the use of nutritional supplements.

There is now a considerable body of evidence from modern nutritional research to confirm the benefits of certain foods as well as some of the vitamins and minerals prepared from them. These are the plants or foods with special properties, or specific substances occurring naturally, which help the body in some of its metabolic processes.

NATURAL 'NORMALIZERS'

There are, in fact, a wide variety of substances that have been found in one way or another to lower the cholesterol level. Perhaps because cholesterol occurs so widely nature has, in her wisdom, provided many agents for its control. But they are not purely for the control of this substance; they have a regulatory effect on a number of other body processes as well. There are very few items in nature which have only one specific function. So many of these substances promote various aspects of bodily function and improve its adaptation to stresses of many sorts. General tonics, such as ginseng, act in this way. They contain what are known as 'adaptogens', ingredients that have a regulatory effect on bodily processes.

Garlic and Onions

The volatile substances of garlic and onions probably account for their proven effect in reducing cholesterol levels. Eat raw onions and garlic regularly, or, if the taste is too strong for your palate, use garlic tablets. Freeze-dried garlic in tablet form is preferable to the capsules, which contain an oil extraction. Garlic tablets taken at night cause very little breath problem, but if you do eat it, you may follow it with raw parsley to combat some of the odour.

Apple Pectin

Pectins are a group of polysaccharides that occur in the intercellular layers of many plants. They are extracted commercially to obtain jelly-like substances used, for example, in the making of jam. Apple pectin is used to make the capsules that contain some natural vitamin supplements, but it is also valuable as a cholesterol emulsifier. The best way to obtain this is to eat raw unpeeled apples. They can be a major constituent of your Fruit Day menu and this is another good reason to include them in a mono-diet such as that referred to earlier.

Oats

Recent reports have confirmed that oatmeal or breakfast oats used on a regular basis can bring about a reduction of blood-cholesterol levels. When porridge eaters were compared with people who did not consume oats in any form, the former were found to have significantly lower blood-fat levels. Oats provide valuable fibre, which takes up excess fats in the intestines and encourages their elimination.

Lecithin

Lecithin has already been discussed in an earlier chapter (page 29). It can be obtained as a convenient supplement in capsule form. The lecithin in these capsules is prepared from the versatile soya bean. One or two capsules may be taken with each meal.

Alfalfa

Alfalfa is rich in substances called saponins (soaps), which bind cholesterol and bile salts in the gut, thus preventing their absorption into the blood.

Alfalfa seeds may be added to salads, fruit salads, or savoury grain dishes. They are suitable for sprouting, which will make their nutrient properties more readily available.

Brewer's Yeast

This is a good source of chromium, sometimes known as the glucose tolerance factor (GTF). This regulates the blood-sugar level, the control of which is important to maintain a proper balance of blood fats.

Incorporating brewer's yeast, available from health food stores, as a food supplement helps to reduce cholesterol levels.

VITAMINS

A number of vitamins play a role in the prevention and treatment of high blood-cholesterol level.

Vitamin E

Vitamin E is the great oxygen-sparer of the body. It reduces the oxygen requirements of the tissues thus improving metabolism all round, but has a particular effect in emulsifying cholesterol and the triglycerides.

The Shute brothers of Ontario, Canada, who did so much pioneering work on vitamin E in the treatment of heart disorders and gynaecological troubles, found it to be an indispensable part of their regime in the management of these illnesses. Because of its tonic effect on the heart, vitamin E should be introduced gradually in cases of high blood-pressure. In other cases 600 International Units per day is an optimum quantity for most people, but larger amounts may be taken under the supervision of a naturopath or doctor. Again, meal times are the best for these supplements. Vitamin E is found naturally in whole grain products and wheat germ.

Vitamin B

Vitamin B is a complex of many vitamins, some of which are used in pharmaceutical doses to lower cholesterol. Nicotinic acid (vitamin B3) and pyridoxine (vitamin B6) are used in this way, but since most of the B vitamins work together it is best to take a good quality B-complex which will improve the ratio of unsaturated to saturated fatty acids in the blood.

Vitamin C

Vitamin C is a major antioxidant nutrient, and because of its role in the maintenance of elastic tissue such as the walls of the arteries, should be included in a supplement programme for the control of cholesterol. It is also an important cofactor in the liver's cholesterol metabolism.

Essential Fatty Acids

The essential fatty acids, referred to in chapter 3, may be taken as supplements. For example, Evening Primrose Oil has been found to lower previously high cholesterol levels. The best sources of essential fatty acids are the foods that contain them, such as oily fish, flax seed oil, sunflower seed oil, and pumpkin and sunflower seeds.

Evening Primrose Oil is available as capsules to supplement the diet and those brands that incorporate fish oils appear to be more effective in reducing arteriosclerosis and coronary heart disease.

AVOID SYNTHETICS

When possible these nutrients should be obtained from the foods which contain larger quantities of them, but under conditions of ill health or potential disorder, such as arteriosclerosis or high cholesterol level, the body's requirements of some vitamins are greater than can be provided in the diet. There is therefore ample justification for the use of supplements provided that they are from natural sources, that is prepared and concentrated from foods in which they are found naturally. Synthetic vitamins, however, are only a chemical imitation of the purified vitamin and because the trace elements and the co-enzymes found with the naturally occurring substance are absent, the biological activity of these artificial substitutes is poorer. Get your vitamin supplements from a reputable health food store. A summary of the most helpful supplements is given in the table overleaf.

You now have many of the elements required to reduce your cholesterol level and gradually to reduce the risk of danger diseases occurring. But if the regime seems too much of a sacrifice of good taste try some of the recipes. They are simple to prepare and wholesome to eat and will restore your appreciation of the natural goodness of real foods.

SCHEDULE OF SUGGESTED SUPPLEMENTS

(in order of importance)

Supplement	Form/Strength	Dosage
Vitamin E	Capsules / 100IU	2 capsules 3 × daily
Vitamin C	Bioflavonoids / 500mg	1 tablet 2 × daily
Garlic	Freeze-dried tablets	3 tablets at night
Vitamin B complex	High potency	1 tablet daily
Evening Primrose Oil	Capsules / 500mg	1 capsule 2 × daily

CHAPTER SEVEN

Recipes

For the person accustomed to the richer fare of the more conventional diet, some of the foods recommended in the previous chapters may seem sparse and uninteresting. In fact they form the basics for what can be a varied and tasty menu, whilst at the same time being more nutritious.

In this chapter you will find recipes to show just how healthy eating can be tasty easting. We only give examples in each basic category; for a greater selection which will widen your scope, you can find many more recipes in books obtainable from health food stores and shops specializing in natural health literature.

Here, then, are recipes for preparation of some of the basic items such as muesli, salads and the main whole grain products.

BREAKFAST DISHES

These recipes are suitable for nourishing breakfasts, but some may also be used as desserts for any meal.

Porridge

- 2 cups water or soya milk
- ½ to 1 cup porridge oats
- Pinch sea salt
- Honey
- Tahini (ground sesame seeds)
- Wheat germ

Place liquid in saucepan and bring to boil. Reduce heat and slowly add oats while stirring. Continue to stir while simmering for 1 2 minutes until porridge is cooked. Serve with soya or skimmed milk and add a little honey, tahini and wheat germ to taste.

Muesli

This will be sufficient for one week. Soak 4 breakfast cupsful of organically grown porridge oats in an equal quantity of water overnight. In the morning add 4 tablespoonsful of wheat germ, 4 tablespoonsful of milled nuts, 4 tablespoonsful of sunflower seeds, 2 heaped tablespoonsful of soya powder, 2 grated apples, 2 pears chopped or grated. Add a tablespoonful of honey or molasses. Mix and serve with yogurt and/or tahini.

Baked Apples

- Large cooking or eating apple
- Seedless raisins
- 2 tablespoonsful of milled nuts

Core the apple, fill the centre with raisins. Place in a little water in a baking dish. Bake for 30 minutes. Serve with milled nuts sprinkled on top. Use a little runny honey to sweeten if desired. Serve with goat's or sheep's milk yogurt.

Apple Purée

- 1 kilo (2¼ lb) apples
- Approximately 1 cupful of apple juice or water
- Runny honey
- Lemon peel or cinnamon
- Milled nuts

Prepare apples, cut into pieces and cook in apple juice or a little water until tender. Rub through a sieve or prepare in a liquidizer. Mix in honey, or lemon peel, or cinnamon. Sprinkle with nuts and place under the grill to brown before serving.

SOUPS

A vegetable stock which can be used when required may be prepared from fresh vegetables or use the water in which vegetables have been cooked for other dishes. Savoury spreads like yeast extracts or vegetable concentrates can be used as stock when it is not possible to use fresh vegetables. Two or three teaspoonsful of the spread to be mixed in half a litre of hot water.

Mixed Vegetable Soup

- Selection of any vegetables in season such as carrots, celery, cabbage, cauliflower, beetroot, leeks, tomatoes, onions, lentils, beans, peas, spinach, potatoes
- 5 tablespoonsful sunflower seed oil
- 2 tablespoonsful wholemeal or soya flour
- Sea salt
- Herbs to flavour

Sauté chopped onions in sunflower seed oil. Add wholemeal flour (this can be mixed in half portion with soya flour if desired). Dilute with vegetable stock. Add conservatively cooked vegetables and allow to simmer for ten minutes. Add brewers' yeast extracts, sea salt, and herbs to flavour.

Carrot Soup

- 2 large carrots
- 1 onion
- 1 tablespoonful wholemeal flour
- 2 oz (50g) sunflower oil margarine (or vegetable oil)
- 1 teaspoonful thyme or other herbs to flavour
- 850ml (30 fl oz) of water
- Sea salt

Dice the carrots, peel and chop the onion, sauté in vegetable oil with herbs for 5 minutes. Stir in flour and add water. Cook gently for 30 minutes. Season with sea salt or yeast extract to flavour.

Onion Soup

- 1 tablespoonful sunflower seed or corn oil
- 2 large onions
- 5 tablespoonsful wholemeal flour
- 2 litres (3½ pt) water
- Sea salt
- Savoury spreads for flavour
- Herbs

Sauté onion in vegetable oil until tender. Add and mix flour, add vegetable stock and sea salt. Cook 30 45 minutes. Sieve if desired and serve with the addition of savoury spreads for flavour.

SALADS

Combination Salad 1

- Half a lettuce
- Watercress
- Cress
- Cucumber
- 2 tomatoes
- Spring onions
- 2 medium carrots
- Mint or parsley
- Milled nuts
- Cottage cheese

Break lettuce into bowl, add watercress, slice cucumber, tomatoes and grated carrots. Garnish with mint and parsley and add cress and spring onions. Sprinkle milled nuts over the salad. Serve with cottage cheese and sunflower seed oil or salad dressing.

Combination Salad 2

- Half a head of green cabbage
- 2 medium carrots
- 2 small onions
- Lettuce
- Radishes

Chop the cabbage finely and add diced radishes and carrots. Serve on a bed of lettuce with dressing. Top with sliced onion.

Winter Salad

- Half a head of cabbage (white)
- 2 or 3 medium carrots
- Half a raw beetroot
- Celery
- 1 green pepper
- 1 onion
- Chicory
- Nuts
- Raisins
- Small portion of cheddar cheese (low fat)

Chop or dice the cabbage, celery, pepper and onions. Grate the carrots and raw beetroot. Mix all ingredients together in a bowl and add milled nuts and raisins. Break chicory on top and sprinkle dressing over the salad before serving.

Apple and Vegetable Salad

- 1 apple
- Celery stalks
- Lettuce leaves or endive or Chinese leaves
- Cucumber
- Nuts

Chop the celery, endive or Chinese leaves and cucumber. Mix in a bowl rubbed with garlic cloves. Add apple slices and sprinkle with milled nuts. Serve with salad dressing.

SALAD DRESSINGS

Lemon and Honey Dressing

- Corn or sunflower seed oil
- Pure lemon juice
- 1 teaspoonful of runny honey
- Herbs
- Sea salt

Mix 75 per cent corn or sunflower seed oil with 25 per cent lemon juice (or apple cider-vinegar), add honey and mix in. Add herbs and sea salt to flavour.

Yogurt Dressing

- 2 or 3 tablespoonsful yogurt
- Lemon juice
- Onion or garlic
- Mixed fresh or dried herbs

Add a few drops of lemon juice to the yogurt and chopped onion or garlic, and whisk thoroughly together with mixed herbs.

SAVOURY DISHES

Savoury Grains

Whole cereal grains such as millet, buckwheat, rye, or brown rice may be used as a savoury dish. Place three to four cupsful of the grains in a saucepan and just cover with water. Bring to the boil, replace the lid, and allow to simmer for 5–10 minutes or longer according to the type of grain. The water should be almost absorbed by the grains. Add grated cheese, chopped onions or mushrooms, flavoured with yeast extracts if desired. Serve with salads or as main dish with two or three conservatively cooked vegetables.

Rice requires longer cooking, generally for 30 40 minutes.

Lentil Savoury

- 225g (8 oz) lentils
- 2 large onions
- 3 tablespoonsful sunflower seed oil or corn oil
- 5–6 peeled tomatoes
- 200g (7 oz) grated cheddar cheese
- 1 large can soya beans (or fresh soya beans which have been soaked for 24 hours)

Cook lentils in a little water (sufficient to cover them) until the water is absorbed. Place in an oven-proof dish. Chop onions and sauté in 3 tablespoonsful of vegetable oil. Add soya beans, tomatoes, and onions, to the lentils. Spread grated cheese over the top. Bake in moderate oven for 20 minutes or until the cheese is brown.

Mushroom and Tomato Savoury

- 225g (8 oz) breadcrumbs
- 225g (8 oz) milled nuts
- 4 tablespoonsful vegetable oil
- 225g (8 oz) mushrooms
- 225g (8 oz) tomatoes
- Sea salt
- Herbs to flavour

Sauté breadcrumbs and milled nuts in vegetable oil, stirring frequently until crisp. Chop the mushrooms and quarter the tomatoes. Sauté these in vegetable oil for 5 minutes. Place a little oil in an ovenproof dish and fill with alternate layers of the mushroom mixture and the nut mixture adding a little sea salt to each layer and herbs to flavour. Top layer should be nut and breadcrumb mixture. Bake for 30 minutes in a moderate oven. Serve with a selection of vegetables.

DESSERTS

Fruit Compôte

- Dried apricots
- Raisins
- Other fresh fruit in season

Soak the apricots in half a pint of water overnight with the raisins. Simmer for 15 minutes. Add fresh fruit suitably chopped or grated. Cook for 5 minutes and serve with milled nuts or almond cream. Sweeten with runny honey or maple syrup if desired.

Stuffed Pears

- 4 pears
- Almond cream
- 1 tablespoonful each of raisins, sliced pineapples, ground walnuts or almonds

Halve the pears and scoop out the cores. Whip almond cream and fold in with raisins, pineapple and milled nuts and place in the centre of the fruit and serve with runny honey or maple syrup as desired.

Orange Jelly

- 1 or 2 cupsful of pure orange juice
- 1 small teaspoonful of agar-agar or portion of pre-prepared carrageen
- Runny honey

Whisk the agar-agar into half the orange juice and add the honey. Heat slowly over a gentle heat until the agar-agar is dissolved. (Do not allow to boil.) Add the remaining orange juice and mix. Pour into individual bowls and leave in a cool place to set. Serve with a sprinkling of milled nuts or almond cream.

Flapjacks

- 3 cupsful breakfast oats
- 1 cupful chopped nuts
- 200g (7 oz) sunflower-oil margarine
- 2 tablespoonsful honey or maple syrup
- 180g (6 oz) Barbados sugar
- 1 tablespoonful cereal coffee substitute

Mix the fat, nuts, oats, coffee substitute, sugar and honey or maple syrup together in a saucepan. Press into a well-greased tin so mixture is 10mm deep. Bake in a slow oven for one hour or until a golden brown all over.

DRINKS

Savoury Drinks

Savoury drinks may be made with low-sodium yeast extract or vegetable concentrates. One teaspoonful should be mixed in a cup of hot water.

Alternatively vegetable juices prepared in a liquidizer may be mixed together. Experiment with combinations of carrots, apples, watercress, celery and beetroot.

Cider Vinegar and Molasses

Mix together one tablespoonful of apple cider vinegar and one dessertspoonful of molasses with warm water.

Lemon and Molasses

Mix together one tablespoonful pure lemon juice with one dessertspoonful molasses and hot water.

Lemon and Honey

Prepare as above using runny honey instead of molasses.

Herb Teas

These may be obtained in tisanes from a health food store or the dried herbs may be used. If the latter method is used, prepare by pouring boiling water over the herb and allowing it to steep for 5 minutes.

CHAPTER EIGHT

Balance

Equilibrium in nature is vital to prevent chaos. The change of the seasons, the cycle of the plants, the ebb and flow of tides are all maintained by some regulating force. In the human body equilibrium is important. The right amounts of the biochemical constituents of our blood are necessary to maintain healthy functions. When we have too much or too little of a particular component our health will eventually suffer – internally a little chaos is occurring.

This is a fundamental fact that as a species we have apparently overlooked. We have tried to improve on nature in so many directions and in our nutritional habits we have moved a long way from it. The chaos of internal disequilibrium is apparent in some of the disease statistics that the epidemiologists have produced for us. The sophistication and speed of the western life-style has necessitated more convenience foods and more refinement and the decline in its quality is painfully apparent to many sufferers from degenerative disorders.

WHY UNREFINED FOODS ARE BETTER

But it need not be of such an appalling and potentially dangerous nature. The balance can be restored by a return to a more natural diet. Wholefoods have the balance of nutrients built into them, hence the importance, for instance, of natural vitamins. Eating food nearer to its raw or whole unrefined state ensures that you get many of the minerals, trace elements, enzymes and vitamins that the body needs to maintain its own internal equilibrium.

This book has attempted to explain how this is possible in a way that can restore cholesterol levels to normal or, for anyone at risk for other reasons, prevent it rising in the first place.

Attaining a balanced diet can be one of the hardest things of all on the path to health. The advice given in this book may well be carried out rigorously and yet may not be suitable in every respect for you as an individual. There are certainly all the basic facts you need on which to model your nutritional programme, but other stresses may be also operating in your life which could offset the most carefully planned diet.

ROLE OF THE EMOTIONS

Consider the effect of emotions on health. Some people regard this as the most important factor influencing even the very physical phenomena, such as cholesterol deposit formation. I believe that a physically healthy, well-nourished body develops a much greater resistance to emotional stress, but there can be no doubt that repetitive anxiety, anger, frustration and other emotional strains do play a potent part in the onset of degenerative disorders.

So, like too much of the wrong type of food, too many negative emotions can have an adverse effect on the working of the liver or the hormone secretions and in a variety of other ways. Eventually the fat metabolism suffers and a breakdown to the smaller fatty globules in the blood doesn't take place in the way that it should.

RELAXATION AND EXERCISE

As well as good food, you need to cultivate the ability to relax, to 'switch off' the stresses of day-to-day life and to allow your body adequate opportunity for rest and regeneration of exhausted adrenal glands and fatigued nerve cells. Rest is also essential, of course, for good digestion of the food you eat. Ensure that you have regular sleep and learn some form of relaxation or even meditation. Tests have been carried out on people who meditate regularly and their metabolism has been found to be improved in a number of ways.

Healthy cells need oxygen, which is carried in the blood. Circulation must therefore be adequate and exercise is an important way of maintaining the blood flow to every part of the body. A small amount of vigorous exercise daily is more beneficial than a burst of intense activity once or twice a week.

Regular jogging, even ten minutes per day, will do more good than a weekend golf or squash session, beneficial though these may be from a recreational point of view. Jogging, or even brisk walking, gradually increases the capacity of the heart, which in turn improves the circulation to every part of the body. The improvement in oxygen supply and drainage of lymph from the tissues prevent the accumulation of toxic metabolites, the waste from bodily functions which can slowly devitalize the cells. Making the lungs work to their fullest capacity also prevents those pockets of stagnant air, which can become a bed of infection.

Other forms of exercise, such as swimming and yoga, are also good. Yoga greatly benefits the breathing mechanism and relaxation but does not improve stamina to the same extent that running or swimming do.

There is definite evidence to show that vigorous exercise lowers the blood-lipid level and a graduated programme, such as jogging, can play a positive role in conjunction with your diet to control cholesterol.

The importance of a balanced and integrated approach was emphasized by a study which found that patients who exercised, practised yoga and ate a vegetarian diet lowered their blood-cholesterol levels and reduced fatty deposits narrowing their arteries within a year. A control group who received normal care, including dietary advice, but without the combination as above showed only a moderate decrease in cholesterol, and arterial blockage was increased.

Exercise, rest and relaxation are fairly obvious requirements of our lives, but it is surprising how few people attain the right balance of them. Moderation and balance are the key words – with moderation in all three you will be some way towards a healthier balance. Perhaps there are other directions in which you could balance your life. Negative emotions, we have seen, can have an adverse effect on health and your attitude will mould your emotions.

EXPLORE NEW WAYS

Obsessions with irrational fears, with diets, or about systems of exercise or any particular cult can lead to disappointment and frustration. There is no single system that can provide all the answers. A therapeutic method survives because it provides something of the truth, but it can never be totally comprehensive in every case. Seek new ways of helping yourself, provided they are in conformity with the constructive principles of natural health.

Consider whether you should obtain professional advice or treatment. Chronic structural problems with your spine may have an adverse effect on the function of internal organs. Osteopathic treatment can gradually correct these. Organ dysfunctions may require the constructive remedial support that can be provided by herbal or homoeopathic medicines. Or there may be imbalance of a finer sort which can only respond to the specialized techniques of traditional acupuncture.

Professional associations of naturopaths, osteopaths, homoeopaths, medical herbalists, and acupuncturists maintain registers of practitioners of these specialities and there may be one in your district.

Your health food store will also be a source of specialist information on nutrition. They generally carry a selection of books and magazines of natural health and also know of practitioners in your area. They certainly have many of the unrefined foods and natural dietary supplements that you require.

Let your attitude be one that seeks the most enjoyment from life, that seizes the opportunities it presents and finds a joy in the simpler pleasures, and you will create the right emotional environment for good health. Achieving balance will become easier and in the framework of a balanced life your diets to control cholesterol will not only do just that, but also maintain your general health and vigour to *live*.

Index

Diets to help
ASTHMA AND HAY FEVER

Suitable for all catarrhal conditions

Roger Newman Turner

Asthma and hay fever can be made worse by eating certain foods, but there are also nutritional guidelines that you can follow to help *manage* the condition. This book explains:

- why some people are prone to asthma or hay fever
- how to cut down on mucus-forming foods
- how to increase your intake of protective vitamins and minerals

It includes basic diets to help control the condition and specific diets for more acute symptoms.

ROGER NEWMAN TURNER is a leading naturopath, osteopath and acupuncturist. He has many years' experience treating a wide range of conditions and runs practices in Harley Street, London and Letchworth, Hertfordshire.

Diets to help
CYSTITIS

Total relief without antibiotics

Ralph McCutcheon

Cystitis is an irritating and often chronic infection of the urinary system which does not always respond to symptomatic treatment through antibiotics

This book offers a full nutritional approach to help restore the body's underlying health and avoid cystitis completely. It explains:

- what causes cystitis
- the complementary treatments that can help
- the importance of a balanced diet
- how to cope with an acute attack

It also includes a selection of basic recipes, advice on mineral intake and suggests which foods will help and which foods to avoid.

RALPH McCUTCHEON is a naturopath, osteopath and acupuncturist with many years' experience treating a wide range of conditions with complementary medicine. His practice is near Belfast, Northern Ireland.

Diets to help
GLUTEN AND WHEAT ALLERGY

Suitable for those with coeliac disease

Rita Greer

Here is sound practical advice on gluten allergy, wheat sensitivity and coeliac disease. It explains:

- what gluten is
- the symptoms of allergy
- a list of 'safe' foods and those to avoid
- useful alternatives to wheat, rye, barley and oats

Also included are basic recipes, emergency menus and facts about coeliac disease.

RITA GREER is an experienced diet therapist and cookery writer. She has many years' experience of coping with a gluten-free diet.

Diets to help
PSORIASIS

The natural way to clearer skin

Harry Clements

The condition of our skin can be greatly affected by the quality of the foods we eat. A poorly controlled diet may aggravate chronic skin conditions like psoriasis, but with the right approach it is possible to clear this ailment once and for all. This book outlines:

- a four week treatment programme
- 'danger' foods and foods to enjoy
- a low protein toxin-free basic diet
- basic recipes and menu ideas

HARRY CLEMENTS practised as a naturopath and osteopath with special interest in skin conditions.

DIETS TO HELP ARTHRITIS	0 7225 2871 X	£2.99	☐
DIETS TO HELP ASTHMA AND HAY FEVER	0 7225 2911 2	£2.99	☐
DIETS TO HELP COLITIS	0 7225 3199 0	£2.99	☐
DIETS TO HELP CYSTITIS	0 7225 2872 8	£2.99	☐
DIETS TO HELP DIABETICS	0 7225 2933 3	£2.99	☐
DIETS TO HELP MULTIPLE SCLEROSIS	0 7225 3239 3	£2.99	☐
DIETS TO HELP GLUTEN AND WHEAT ALLERGY	0 7225 2910 4	£2.99	☐
DIETS TO HELP PSORIASIS	0 7225 2929 5	£2.99	☐

All these books are available from your local bookseller or can be ordered direct from the publishers.

To order direct just tick the titles you want and fill in the form below:

Name: _____

Address: _____

_____

_____ Postcode: _____

Send to; Thorsons Mail Order, Dept 3, HarperCollins *Publishers*, Westerhill Road, Bishopbriggs, Glasgow G64 2QT.

Please enclose a cheque or postal order or your authority to debit your Visa/Access account –

Credit card no: _____

Expiry date: _____

Signature: _____

– up to the value of the cover price plus:
UK & BFPO: Add £1.00 for the first book and 25p for each additional book ordered.
Overseas orders including Eire: Please add £2.95 service charge. Books will be sent by surface mail but quotes for airmail despatches will be given on request.

24 HOUR TELEPHONE ORDERING SERVICE FOR ACCESS/VISA CARDHOLDERS – **TEL: 0141 772 2281.**